IN A PASTURE WITH

PALOMINOS

IN A PASTURE WITH

PALOMINOS

JOAN STEPP SMITH

TEBOT BACH • HUNTINGTON BEACH • CALIFORNIA • 2010

Cover image: Tony Stromberg

Layout and design: Melanie Matheson, Rolling Rhino Communications

ISBN 13: 978-1-893670-37-2

ISBN 10: 1-893670-37-6

Library of Congress Control Number: 2009941520

A Tebot Bach book

Tebot Bach, Welsh for little teapot, is A Nonprofit Public Benefit Corporation which sponsors workshops, forums, lectures, and publications. Tebot Bach books are distributed by Small Press Distribution, Armadillo, Ingram, and Bernhard De Boer.

The Tebot Bach Mission: Advancing Literacy, Strengthening Community, and transforming life experiences with the power of poetry through readings, workshops, and publicatons.

This book is made possible by a grant from The San Diego Foundation Steven R. and Lera B. Smith Fund at the recommendation of Lera Smith.

www.tebotbach.org

For Erik Lee Preminger

ACKNOWLEDGMENTS

My very special thanks to David St. John for his help and many reassurances while I wrote the manuscript.

I'd also like to thank Susan Terris and CB Follett whose innumerable kind and perfect efforts helped bring my work to the page.

My gratitude for their tenacity, caring and unfailing enthusiasm goes to Rose Black, David L. Smith, Sharon Lais Mohorovich, Naomi Mann, Helen Cassidy Page, Margaret Kaufman, Julia Hansen, Carol Levine, Carole Piasente, Persis Knobbe, Sandra Lloyd and Douglass Smith, James Karen and Alba Francesca, Terry Ehret, Tom Jenks, Carol Edgarian, Robert Works Fuller, Kris Saknussemm, William David Jenkins and dearest Rupert Hine for that sweet measure of early encouragement everyone needs.

I can never fully thank my Cloudview Poet friends who have been reading this collection over the years as it evolved.

CONTENTS

RINGS AND BARS

FAMILIAR ANIMALS

OPERA GOD

INTRODUCTION

JOAN STEPP SMITH'S *In A Pasture With Palominos* is a one of the most exciting and original collections of poetry in recent years. Conceptually brilliant, verbally breath taking and stylistically innovative, Joan Stepp Smith's poetry invigorates and recalibrates all of the complex issues of art and experience. The pleasures of these poems are many, including the discovery of the poet's complex narrative architectures and high-wire verbal antics [calisthenics?] that both surprise us and are able to alter a poem at moment's notice. There are elements here of high farce and serious philosophical meditation, of intimate memoir and classical ode. Sometimes elegantly discrete and sometimes operatically grand, Joan Stepp Smith's poetry can shift at every turn and bend the mind to new and sometimes alarming directions [and dimensions].

There is a sweeping cinematic grandeur here, and at times, a tremor of worldly anxiety runs the course of a whole passage. It is this combination of disquiet and bravado that I admire so deeply in Joan Stepp Smith's work, along with her fiercely inventive language play. Once in a while a poet emerges who leaves us shaken with her accomplishments and wisdoms. *In A Pasture With Palominos* is a book of wonder.

— *David St. John*

RINGS AND BARS

SKILLS AND DRILLS

Here, the well-hung Katydids spare no pulse-time jabber
— irksome, they run rampant down in our lower meadow
until we set it on fire and my summer needs to be playing hop-scotch
and he needs that infernal gas can, our passports, some umbrage in his pockets
jangling — Me? I'm just learning about Quetzalcoatl and insects,
the ones who upchuck their young, collusion and the grim news
it is illegal to pick a California Poppy
—Mrs. Pacquette said you could actually go to jail for it.

She won't see them etching rufus ampersands into the cradle
of my back and yellowing up his knees down by Equisetum Bend
where he takes me to stand in homage to our flames
after Grandfather's funeral, after being angry the apple orchard was losing us
so much money, how each piece of fallen fruit called out its crimes
he said, just before the rains come . . . Small warning to the still
ripe hanging [by whatever luck God gives them]
they are not so rotten yet.

And, walking the old meadowland today, I take my dog,
Jezebel. She fears no poppy laws, no unmitigating mosses
or if ticks suck her blood with gusto not malice,
when I return here to venerate those who have loved me at my lowliest
and a flock of blackbirds springs up from nowhere
leaving the pig grass swaying into a virtuosity of parables,
and she won't sense the presence of a snake eating a smallish rabbit
[more-or-less-dead] is still
fighting.

Instructions on How to Spell 'Jam'

First — know when the night train leaves. Look left down the tracks for the
boy's early life. Observe he grows gills before whiskers, on each cheek, in the
shape of 'J's and often sees himself lying on his back at the bottom of the lake,
the lake behind Burt Carson's Creamery, the lake people call The Killer, where
he, his step-father, and three boy cousins practice spelling and dream of cutting
a canal to Rome. 1966: Trail him. It's August and always under the same
weeping willow. Clutch your stomach. Watch as neighborhood cats get hung
by their tails alive for insurance, for something too hard to speak of and

breathe: deep . . . deeper . . . deeper still, to do certain things watching out for
others, but don't turn your back, screaming cats can claw right into a brain,
rip out the throat of some forty years down the road and if this happened to
a man you could not love enough, collect that August 'A', add it to the fish
hook 'J' from one of his pliant gills, and looking at this man you've known
from the time he was this boy and you could not hold a pencil under your
breasts, ignore it if he says you are driving him to go watch the leaves come
filtering down. Take up piano, play Liszt, tell him you're not made for marrying
in a house without a staircase, the 'M' you need is not coming from 'marriage'
and don't go dwelling on schools of finicky fish, either . . . the way they
picked his eyelids clean. Lessons in collusion have to be digested elsewhere,
and, if, you find yourself unsure whether you are angry enough or smarter
than that, be sure to follow these steps: Find a book of matches, smoke out
the macabre 'M'. Go ahead. Add it to the 'J' and the 'A' and face it. This is
your 'JAM' — Yes, but

all the stars are finally beaming in his direction, just as they had that day he
won his first spelling jam away from you. 7th grade — Remember?

4

'Controversy' was the word to clench it. Still, what thesaurus parses why a boy's life gets lost in a controversy all its own, under a weeping willow by a lake you would surely hate to drain for its secrets now — Yes, he taught you only one 'S' goes into insouciance and those two cozy 'F's siamesed in ineffable, nonchalant as lovers, aren't holding hands, they're handcuffed for execution.

JAM? Relax. Dream of standing in the ocean surf swaying between your legs. He's with you and you are whispering *I loved being your dictionary of choice.* Look up from time to time, watch for Heavenly Bodies coming into their brief sparkle; recall his eyes, opening the way you loved — Oh, those fare-thee-well eyes, blue as blue-blue rum, murky as omens.

COMBINATIONS EXCEEDING BORDER MARKINGS

Rain freezes the streets. What time is it? I'm home.
I live here; he thinks when ice makes the trees heavy,
the lawn a bit more ephemeral. Gestalt of the fumble,
double-dipped keys in the locks of their dark house, that flummox,
      passing through a portal to find oneself
      clueless as to why he is willing to be robbed.
Except, the 'other' woman, then,
      the one from his 'other' world,
      ignored the rich tautness in the pit of his stomach,
      gladly misconstrued his disappointment,
      that shoved back look,
      that somewhere so blank his fingerprints must be missing;
      that in case of his murder, investigators wouldn't know
      he'd been so despised,
all the while dancing in the cross hairs of so little mercy,
      his so-so daughters will ask her [not their mother]
         how best to dump their married men.

Do you think anyone cares?

They wanted answers, Jacques.

        What about before we were born?
        Was there a history?
        Any sign?

Daughters' questions: Hot ash on frill,

noose burns gathering throat flesh

around what must stay unspoken,

burning the script, burning while comparing wrinkles

over a glass of Punt e Mes, four women, after his funeral, so diffuse
by now, their topics slosh Diane de Poitiers's politesse into Catherine
De Medici's venom into small dogs barking, stitched inside belly shells of disemboweled
collaboratuers . . . *Ah, those pregnant women from Algiers,*

the mother says, who wants the tone to shift. *1957: Imagine this.*

Set on fire by zee French, no less. Le pur et l'impur . . .

ruff-ruff [she makes those dog sounds of hers] . . . At his funeral
she wants to shine her memory on atrocity, wants to talk too much . . .
Torture isn't very efficient, if you're used to it, she says.

And, suppose, if one isn't? The oldest daughter says.

Cherie, you mean, capitulate? Jamais!
One shall need to die either way, will they not?

Hook & Loop Mother of the Bride

After 'I do' blossoms me.
Whatever I've done tapers her.
Maybe, she weeps. For this.
A missing vista, perhaps?
Her Astarte lost in an only daughter,
mincing princess steps down the aisle
that led her head-on into a wall.

SWING-SET

Soon, out of the womb 'down there' is nuance.
It guides you, like a legality, like your own breathing,
in and out of overtone, hardcore hodgepodges,
those inklings near sacrosanct beyond breakfront
negligees and neo-negligence leading the good life.
Isn't it romantic? Wasn't it morbid? Watching
the cleaning girl rush to catch his car,
her fine-boned feet skipping soft down the stairs, after him,
after he'd left your bed, still damp,
her trotting alongside his black Bavarian car,
you watching her tapping on his blue-tinted window,
him lowering it just a slit, just the barest invitation for her
willing fingers to enter, and like little arrows make contact
with a man who has no clue how much you've watched his starving
girl, that pulling back of her hand from the pinch of a future
choking, that sucking on her insensible fingers, not knowing
how easily you could have taught her to tip them with poison.

Floor Work

Startled by his voice
she steps from the shower
half smiling. What did you say?
He rushes to hold her
wearing her favorite suit,
his hand strumming-warm
on her back, the way she likes it,
now, the perfect canvas for a butcher
knife: *You were it*
and when he says it again
it sinks in, scratchy
gabardine, starched cuffs rough
all of him rough to the floor.

Shhh, he says — *Shhh.*

But, what can be pushed into this?

GREEN-EYED CATECHISM WHIPSAWS GRIPS & LEVERS

You sure? You really sure you want to kiss me on the mouth again?
Here, near the hemmed-in ground without some stratagem,
some arr-u-gah, or hoo-ah, or ooh-la-luau serving contrapposto eel?

One opulent muscle for dither — You sure,
you really sure you want to kiss me here,
me, your green-eyed catechism in a wooing mood?

Fine, then. Stroke my green cool belly, let my dipstick
eyes fertile as lava light the black nights
you grow suspicious, doppelgangers with real girl legs

stroll the beaches with him. Real man paranoia?
Isn't that 4 a.m. when the tide switches sides?
Aren't you begging me then to sing for you

with my wild summer mouth and diminished plush
notes, to pinken your poitrine with, to whipsaw,
to pet, to polish your leather of hummingbird tail?

So — Kiss me. Let me deadhead your scales back to lamé . . .
No. She cannot. She would see her death begin:
See herself being shipped to the cannery

in a net with sand dabs, glinty banderillas, chaos
clumped at her neck. Armada of twitches:
Shipwreck:

11

Face it, the Green Eyed Catechism says,
Anxiety is shipwreck. Shipwreck is mass.
Mermaids are whiff

and do not need another over-particular epicure
or the sea another ruse, here, near the hemmed in ground —
So, kiss me. Together we'll stop the ones with Pavlov between their lips,

the blonde rock star who sings of crème du Longchamps,
the others who shape shift their Artemis
to the sunny side of Mademoiselle Australopithecus — Kiss me.

Haven't I had my tongue down your fear, licked your hindsight, and hinterland
given him all your power? Pardon? Really, you think he's going to need you
to get him back down the gorges to the river?

Only you can guide him along the narrow tributary to the blind bird sanctuary?
Can't you let that be here? Here, in the Marsh with me? No?
Skip the kissing, then, because, you kiss me, I flood his people.

None will I spare. You won't survive, either. Not in my green waters.
Not in my chartreuse veins ticking.
Forget having the copse behind your back.

Forget Aristotle. Forget the fine line between passion and permutation.
Personally, I prefer my women-fish dangerous and, with that,
the mermaid dives and the clouds turn left leaving the sky,

just as the moon slides its white polka dot into blackwater fern
her face emits a greenish glow, green as the worry
she cannot go deep enough to release

the sting of its rapier eel teeth, eight tentacles,
latched onto the rise of flesh right below her last rib:
Its voice in her head growing louder: *You've returned to me often yet,*

now, you must flee? Do please remind me: Didn't you preen in my wounds?
Didn't your blood turn mine green? Haven't we eaten together
on your blue sequined blanket laughing? Or, was it gunfire

causing the loons to yodel last night before dropping out of the Heavens?
Over in the bracken, that aardvark the loons fell on,
wasn't it suffocated in the pummeling?

And about those madcap ants escaping its snoot?
Suppose their surprised exodus will come to mean nothing? And, the waters?
Tell me. Would they have risen today, had we never kissed?

LANDING PIT

Something sacramental happens
in Mummenschanz of the insane mother,
pure and hopeless, detail-by-detail,
the two of you, cohorts
woven out of the same cloth afraid
your voices cannot be told apart.
Of course, you weep.
She is already in you.

FLIGHT ELEMENTS WHEN ONE OF THEM SPLITS

She sees herself walking with Noah.
They're on top of a mountain,
in the middle of an ocean. Clamped over hers,
his hairy hand urgent as they struggle
to climb a rocky path, the Ark now stuck
in the crook of a giant redwood
animals leaving two-by-two:
Antelope, Achtung, Armadillo, Baby Doll Sheep,
            Boer Goat, Bear, Brahma, Buffalo
— Bovine extraordinaire, Elsie after her kind. Camel
capybara, caribou, Cocteau, cougar, Cortazar, Cleopatra
[actually Tony Perkins] . . .Two of every sort,
and every creeping thing of the earth, after its kind,
mélange and malediction except, nowhere
her beloved bats with their tender tempers
borne upside down. *Bats. Here bats. Wake up.* Noah
punches the side of her head. *Watch the road, stupid.*
Hanging off her cerebellum now —
bats, like stalactites, waking at a very bad time:
antsy bats, dropping down bats, on the ground bats,
figments crawling with Edith Piaf clawlets — Dark red
pointy sharp, claws to forde early questions: Should I stay awake?
Should I play dead? Who is this sawed-off Natalie Wood
dreaming on bad radar with the unshaved legs?
Doesn't Noah like his women smooth?
[tedious unlikelihoods]
            The mud is so slippery now,

15

each time she falls,

      Pick up your feet, you dumb galoot, Noah scolds

shooting a look death might use . . . that infinitude,

that self-portrait she'd rather not take to heart,

when out of the blue, circling

in descending halos above his head,

one blue fruit bat in full riding regalia:

sterling collar points, buck stitched chaps,

fringe and cuckoo conchos jangling

and, on its dinky bat feet red ostrich

bull-doggers [Tony Llama's]

rosetta spurs, chrome ones whirring

[Buzz saws is what they are] efficient,

enough to ream out Noah's eyes. First, the left.

Then, the right and, when he's blind,

the dreamer can run. She's running, rising

and flying now right flank above the deluge

in formation with cattle-punching bats

the one's good at using words like 'hubris' and 'slam dunk'.

These bats are bound for the most delectable cave, they say.

But, she's not fooled, she knows

bats don't come out during the day,

not out of the sleeping mouth of the cave,

where, oddly enough, Billie Holiday is washing dishes

in her housecoat, belting out *'Some Other Spring'*

Bitchin' tune, ain't it? The lead bat flying next to her says:
Bardot won't let Billie sing anything else.

Bardot? [Bardot with all the dogs, Bardot?]

No sooner it's said when a husky bat voice rings out,

  Yep — BB — same one — the recluse who loves
    the shadow of what's past more than the actuality of what was.

A philosophical breed — blue bats — amassed against a sapphire sky
leaving Noah's provenance behind
and leaving the world a blue precisely the color
Italian Jews paint their houses and Moslems will not
despite how impressive it is at repelling flies,
fly eggs, strangely, the color of this dream
with no crossroads Dark Ages ago
eager to be in such a place,
a dreamer not knowing how hard it will be
to put her make-up on.

CROSS POSITIONS

On fire on fire on fire on fire on fire on fire
on fire . . . Why fire ? Stick asks carrot dangling
arch-backed the day Miss White taught her
about egg tempera and at the climax, broke an egg.

It was not unbearable.
There was no better life.
Art would be what was needed.
She sees it every day in her garden,

mornings from up on the balcony
she lets the neighbor watch as she throws pebbles
into the summer pond below. Sisyphus,
her eldest Goshiki Koi, doesn't mind.

Unduped by the meteoric, he's used
to garden clocks rolling uphill, in ticks
chiming and framing, a widening mystery
inevitably kept distant as sorrow,

beyond solace, it seems. Even Chickadees,
without a concept for brooding, vie to nest
between her breasts as she paints, and the few she lets
do so, fidgety, as past lives on pink pillows.

Recall Sisyphus abhors dwelling on past lives. He prefers
hollering: *embark, embark.* His frenetic fish fanfare

causing Chickadees to flit Gilberto sans Jobim,
like a bit of samba, *ay caramba*

unaccustomed to what can be lacking:
bliss in missing beats, largesse patina'd with petty
crush of a buckling astonishment, beneath a man,
O man, this becomes intolerable. The Lord Krishna said so.

Intolerable to remember past lives. Isn't that what He said?
Not the rickety business climbing down ones memory.
Said so to Arjuna. Praising forgetfulness,
she taps her canvas, pebbles gone, Chickadees gone

painting and over-painting in her plush public way:
eglantines, prickle rose and crinoline petal'd
pips daubed thick as far flung flesh:
pent up boondoggle hives

painted scorched shut, yellow coronas,
their blow-torched azure edges,
rims to a gruesome certainty
these briar worlds are tinder-ripe.

Chickadees are going to be singed,
with no clue before the match is struck,
to clear the cleavage,
vamoose the posthumous,

scram the spillzone: pond - penance -
hot-cha-da-de-cha canvas and, so on
and on, from where what are you now
is where there are no words.

PARALLEL BARS

They met by chance near St. Tropez,
     around midnight
     walking. He couldn't sleep.
     She was in love with a Jesuit.

Schubert's Trout (loud and maniacal)
     rushed through sea-charged air
     as if shot from the mood of a gun.

"Such great music, such great musicians. How great to be
     hearing this in the middle of nowhere," she said.
     "Music can be anywhere it is made
     . . . like a *hiss* behind the knee," he said.

Soon, she understood, as she had made and unmade nowhere
     in her mind many times before hearing his story,
     and why she hesitates, even now, to make her bed.
     Not from loathing the should of it, or the mindlessness of it,
     or the desire for order, but for the lessons
     she could leave behind in the crumple.

Sure, she relives her walk near St. Tropez,
     those hours spent with a stranger who survived Dachau
     playing 'The Trout' in his head: migratory, ecstatic,
     magical in all parts, note-by-note,
     non-stop for two years

and delusion was not what he suffered
      and why neither ever speaks of
      a night taken as far as they could
      or why the heart cannot be talked about.

FAMILIAR ANIMALS

Qualia in the Nick of Rhyme

Brown as bent bark over a muddy path, eyeless frogs
live as caryatids squinched under horses' hooves
same way the forbidden holds up the mind:

Beastigial incompletes: how they hitch to experience, conjugate
ha-ha from hovel from contextual fickle of a family house —
the one in question had no bedroom doors, no visible louse,

three ivory bisque bidets — American Standards. An aberrance
the way a mind decodes consequence, uses fresh water to drain
and refill the porcelain before it stains vermillion and synapses fire,

enfilade the *where were you* to the *I was there*
to *the puny peculiar.* Observe: Under the toaster, the old yellow lizard,
he's still there, pensive and recollecting blue overalls slipping

off the heart of an ass, caught in chromium silence, picture
in a picture. Well, viva la sheen, this business of polishing over the years,
the limbic brain imbroglios an incredulity easy as the fencer dinks an épée,

lops off a tid-bit of ear to scare and to spare a sorry soul at once.
That lizard under the toaster — He's well past all unpleasurable
sense of doubt as a younger lizard he'd felt, unable to integrate the facts.

Namely, certain vulnerables in their magnitudes can squeal
[or not]. It's a bit like chess. Nimsovich, the great tactician
understood the passed pawn has a lust to expand

25

bored as planets in need of a change of orbit. No damning abstraction.
Just one of the mind's greatest foibles, the way it opts for redemption,
eager to travel the most frail, most radiantly treacherous thread

in a line of logic on its way to somewhere sweeter and safer
before Herr pie-in-the-sky picks up His breathing,
has time to devour each new gullible self.

Qualia (singular: "quale") are most simply defined as the properties of sensory experience by virtue of which there is something it is like to have them. The essence of something, i.e. personhood or darkness. These properties are, by definition, epistemically unknowable in the absence of any direct experience of them; as a result, they are also incommunicable.

CANARY BEFORE CANCER

Rather than visit, my mother says, *Don't talk.*
Click on Oprah. It's a gas pretending
she's got me on the show [Why would Oprah want you

as a guest, I ask] and her black marimba eyes stop
dancing, those two obsidian planets cut in
same as when she decided I got cooties

from the Church Bazaar and not those other things
from home. *Get the Hell out of here*, she scoffs,
pushing the hospital cat off her lap.

Thank God, I got my pizzazz still.
I make meow sounds, seduce the cat back
to my lap. Mother adjusts her new Eva Gabor wig.

Christ, you pick up a bug nowadays,
it don't got to be curtains. You'll just order me up
some stem cells and BINGO — Right, Oprah?

RED BACK SALAMANDER

Digging weather:
Mongrel dogs: the *ones* who rumple beds,
hoard their bones in double curtained rooms
where the windows need duct tape to mask in fog
and opening splints to see outside
where the leaves have been on the trees too long
and birds bitch they've got the wrong teeth
for sucking burning rubber — Time has to pass like this
until a tulle breeze arrives entirely uninvited.

She'd just left her pin-dropping sleep
the night the Red-Back Salamander entered
to rest on her unused pillow, dust-caked
and nearest her outside world and her black
table phone maybe she hadn't answered enough
letting it fuse its opulent saxophone body
and bullish-cabochon crude tones to her cold
red-as-a-river after-massacre shyness,
that moonlight after crickets fall asleep.

Detail-by-detail. Like declension in a conch shell, its ear-hole:
and the eye, gateway iris flexing and contracting: Vista
through a keyhole to signs and eons, this trap work,
this breathing behind the lungless ethic ruling salamanders.
And, how easily now she understands they can rob air off
those who sleep too much with their stilettos on.
Falsified memory: mishmash and aftermath

from stairway to the cliff. Falsified memory:
How often must one call up the vicious
innocence of animals nearing death?

EPISTLE: DEAR MARY, DEAREST PIG

Carl Chessman got gassed the day you squashed your young
against the pump house. Six piglets snuffed
he'd been planning to show. Me? I was the first
to find them curled into stiff C's like massive shrimp
clumped in Mother's shrimp clover she'd smuggled back from Agrigento,
"Trifolium Incarnatum, hardiest forage cover in Christendom,"
He said that, Mary. To you, the most disconsolate pig I'd ever seen,
said it in the spirit of the dead watching,
said it cradling our favorite, the black and white pinto,
him letting you lick and tap it with your boogery nose,
him and you, Mary, and the adorable Stan Unusual.
He named him Stan Unusual.
But what does having a sense of humor matter to the little deaths
held up in those bone dry hands of his like a cocktail before mass?
Mary, am I not already fixated on death and hands:
filial hands, filibuster hands, full-fledged hands,
fandango hands, farrier hands, farmer hands, fiduciary hands,
flotsam hands, all the fraternatural fracases of a father's hands
bearing silence to a moist cheek like your little dead pig.
Mary, no matter what he'd done, no matter what we'd done,
hands are pulling on me at the drawback like waves cuddle
and punch us up at once, like the whore and the love she inspires,
she's sold before. Oh, Mary . . . It was more than about hands.

Go figure. For Stan, he actually wept
               and did not punish the mother.

DAO OF TAXIDERMY

When afternoons get sorry as spoon meat, they go to San Francisco
after, to see plays, juicy ones: *Tartuffe* — *Hair* —
Albee's, *A Delicate Balance* . . . the brand new *Mame* . . .

or they see a movie or, sometimes, visit the Natural History Museum
for one of his special tours of the stuffed animal room,
that buck-toothed friend of his, the curator, lifting glass cases

to let her touch velvety furred moles, *Mokelumne Moose*,
the gnarly backed *Haberdasher Hogs* of lower Mt. Diablo
in a ring around *Marmota Vancouverensis*,

the little Whistle Pig, a member of the squirrel family
she is sure is trying to speak to her, stranded there, poor thing,
riddled with museum beetles, the small face, vigilant, in a way

that makes a person wonder what exactly she was seeing
at the end, before the phony eyes got wired in,
her filthy forefeet and fossorial claws

designed for digging up roots and running away
would be full of dirt and silence, too,
even if someone had decided to leave her alone.

SNAKE REDUX

Paris: It is Easter. Pink steams Eastern windows.
Her lover blooms proverbial pink elbows,
interstitial kisses slow as church smoke
graze her pink closed lids. But, she sees through
to someone else's face: Hoe in hand, she hears
her father saying *if you're gonna cloud up, don't look
then,* that kindly wince [as always] too late —
Pilloried in the white picket fence, a Cotton Mouth,
six wooden eggs lodged firmly in its stomach, the inscrutable
severed head, one cold aspic eye, sunward, brain-dead
body writhing, not a foot from where another pink
head got lost, back when a snake killer said
That'll teach ya — Happy Easter, sucker.

IMPETUS BUILDS A LANGUAGE [IN A PASTURE WITH PALOMINOS]

Listen. You had a gut ache. We blame her cioppino.
Couldn't have you barfing on old Dick and Jane—Right?
I pick you up. We do the mayonnaise route, I buy you a bag of carrots
from that guy up the Caldecott she likes me to get the torpedoes off.
Talk slow. Start with we saw the fawns again on Fish Ranch Road.
You were hounding me to swing you past the canyon.
You just had to feed the mare by the smoke stack out there I'd seen up for sale.
She knows you're gaw-gaw for Palominos.
Tell her barbed wire did it — Period.
I'll say I told you twice not to crawl through that fence.
No — Better, you say, the mare chased you. You fell.
Criminy, stop it about the dress. Your mother sews.
She'll mend it if you tell her. That's it. Oh, oh —
Mention you love Palominos and you want that filly
. . . the one I'm getting you come Easter,
provided everybody stays chipper and can keep their big-little-trap shut.
Capeche, Kimosabe?

Capeche was a vetch field east of Pleasant Hill
where horses had been grazing since Spanish land barons settled there
a hundred years before. *Capeche* was a desert
hideaway found raising a Palomino named Butter Pat
you could bottle feed through two colics, teach to bow
      without begging for sugar, in the sweet grass,
      behind the tack house,
her hiccup filly breath the visiting saint
liable to vanish for the slightest non-compliance.

33

[*Now come the feelings far beyond the subject*]

The crucifix: After the lights go out: Inside the house
purple pubic hair growing from the Savior's crotch
in liable gobs, liable to stain the glacier of liable white carpet
purple. Stark and arch — Easier to imagine half a wayward hula skirt
not the liar's paradox. That would come later,
       sitting in the concert hall, hearing Schoenberg's Violin Concerto
       needing a soloist with a sixth finger,
being played anyway by a violinist less endowed.
The 'unplayable' unfolding: That open
country where all the bridges become their names:
Masquerade, Town Crier, Clockwatcher,
      The Span of the Already Strangled . . .

Of course, Blackmailer's and Bootlicker's bridges are here, too.
But why admit taking them on the way into Truth City
      unless in a mood to be harsh?

DREAM IF THE OWL STILL CALLS

Ever read Gulliver's Travels ?

Her words summon a certain instinct, that ringing
bell in brains signaling the scope of danger at hand.

Didn't think so, she says skipping
a kiss across each cheek
while he fantasizes a reprieve
while she checks the strength of her work,
releasing a French twist, holding the hair
pin in her right palm like toll money.

Your tip, she says.
Unamused, he watches
her left wrist, as a roll of gaffer's tape hides her watch
as a fragmentary look of bewilderment plays quickly over his face.
Something? Of course, you'd like to say, 'something'
but this is impossible as acquiring a fetlock or a pastern.

Later, in barest light, very close to his right ear,
she will whisper *the race to observe is Number 8,*
        and begin to draw infinity signs in the inch of air just
        above his eyes with that pin.
It is into this uncertainty, muffled clicking noises, indistinct as debarked
dingo mingle with the pillowy collisions of wet hair
slapping against starched sheets. Several blood soaked goose feathers
        stuck in the stubbly crook of his neck flutter

ruby red in a platinum sunray slanting
its fine line through the room's drawn curtains.
Dramatic vestiges. Bloodlust. Flashback: baby owl
rescued the day President Kennedy got shot,
the one he shot for insurance. *Ain't it the limit?*
Unconsoling words.

          Unconsoling as her retreating nakedness
should baffled detectives revive him in time. For them,
he might speak High Dutch or High-Handed Horse.
Adept at neighing intonations, once, how much will he readily divulge?
He could not live without the simulacrum of loathing, and
a gobbling greed for the smell of Aqua Velva on her breath?

[*But, if you want to dream so badly, why not let him live ?*]

COMPANY POLICY ON BREEDING ISOLATES

Self rescue devoid an argot for sin means
blue-butted macaques with no mind warp
for Hell get born, play hard, trust, and fall.

Do they tippy-toe up to some morass or demur a splurge,
recoil like the tide, decline to plunge headlong? No.
They're game to bathe, and do so singing, en Français:

Regardé: La mer, La mer. C'est une douche labas . . . Do it frisky,
manage to be clean, to freely wash in the tarnished sea
where a pleasure is found in some swimming, too.

Fickle as saliva, riptides may carry a carelessness
and a macaque might find itself floundered beyond a reef, swimming
for the flicker of a cruise ship — a small reprieve simpering

on the horizon, minuscules, the pin-prick people, cheery
there on iddy-biddy decks, their teensy-tiny hands waving
mosquitoish, ethereal, Godlike voices ghazalish:

> Hey, monkeys . . .
> Lookie here, monkeys
>
> . . . dufus apes,
> stupnickel apes . . .

They're drowning, dumb monks . . .
Honey, check out the drowning monks . . .

egging on a swimming out of luck and, for what?
A pleasing pitch, a come hitherness scaring stories to unwind
in crooked lines for daredevils on parade,

[blue-butted macaques, in this case] exhausted,
though, enough will make it home to take their chances
with cat-o-nine crocs famished, waiting for them back where they left

stuck in their own rut, having correctly calculated
what cannot breathe under water or pick its place of corrupt
with fewer predators, higher ground, sweeter water,

unlike a woman might choose sweeter water
let it flow like prayer down her throat
with or without a good grip on gluttony:

for grand possibility, for simple quench — Underscoring what?
Nothing. Except, crocs and women dice up their boring cuisine,
inclined to devour the occasional uncooked monkey

all breathy and chump-like seize the hapless
at that point- of-no-return when a mouth just
opens for the Sturm und Drang of yum,

yum where the circus starts as darkness drops
in crocs' labyrinthine guts, scrumptious
mush: macaque mélange — a yum next to a heart that purrs

in a palisade of ribs' acidic porridge rock-a-bye-baby crib
ex post facto pabulum of the about to be eaten alive — woe [not whoa].
Look, it isn't meant to be pretty. Of course not, Predicament says.

Neither is it meant to be ugly, asserts Raised Eyebrow,
delicately arched. To which, Rigor Mortis pooh-poohs them both
in its inimitable stiff hiss — *Sheesh.*

BETWEEN ICE COLD REASON & A HANKERING FOR STING

Think Fay Wray: Clingy but what genius,
making her attacker be her handiwork
or, was it her masterstroke, her hustler,
her hostel in a gloom of skyscrapers, her S-O-S
playing out the hand of hoopla and doom,
for ecstasy, for wanting to be persuaded,
for pretty-please, portion-control, no-palm-is-an-island
for the love of even the uncuddliest gorilla,
in its thrall she will overcome a fear of heights —

Amazing Fay Wray. Who ever really hands it to her . . .
manipulating King Kong like that, risking a fall
and why is Autumn messy and brownout unappealing
or any maiden voyage on the dingy of death
about to set sail through thinning light
when the bees are beginning to freeze — Tilt:
unless, they've grown nuts. Wait —

Nutted up bees are another story:
According to Vitto [*Torpedo Nose*] Vespa.
A Well-Nutted Bee is a damn-ass-wicked-bee
tree-smart clever-as-any-Catholic-cat-on-a-drainboard-come-fish-Friday.
He's proof, Vespa says, *that dicking with appetite never pays*
You got to be a do-anything-on-empty sort of bee.
Mindful, always, your stinger has one time privileges;
and your hunger, not your hang-up for honey,
the better snark to worship

No matter if it means you eat your worker bees,
or take pot-shots at sacred cows
or run off your bee-keeper
> *lapsing back into his quiet work-a-day world.*
No free nappin' in the shade —
You live to expand your territory,
vex whole continents
into pondering the prospect of mass
stinging invasions. Yes, if you have to — Cognoscenti and
cut-throats notwithstanding — Nobody's immune.

[That's the buzz.]

SYNESTHESIA

Colors and Patterns Settle Their Various Duties

Shirt-tail crink, a luster like old bacon tastes
beneath the mother's orchid, frowning
       down from its window case oasis — Lucky it:
       Hot and moist, its shape of milk smells
purple bruise of Arpege kitten cock triggerish,
pearly petals with pink glitches such days are now
       prey of a genuine need to know why
1 remains chartreuse
9 bluest of blues
6 a not so thrilling tongue-red like
5 on fire was the whole inflagrante year
       — 1965 — back draft — a bit like Horseradish
       chewed and embarrassed
[Maybe, it's where the creative work starts
adapting to pleasure] Hush … Listen. This is not gibberish.

It's the prism abstract language fogs,
under plots skanked beneath chiaroscuros
Potemkin Villagizing why no story worth telling is
captured in the dirt with ice plant paint.
       Darling?
       Yes, dear.
       'Garbo' in Italian means grace.
       Since when? After it stopped meaning garbage collector?

Maybe he thinks Karenina's soul is a match for her face?
Maybe she wanted the world
       to need more dusk and less dotage?
       If that orchid ever slept or told
how many times a valiant vermouth got chunked
at his head, slashed a cheek
       fat from too much cereal and peaches, is unclear,
       red rivulets filling the minute ruby lake of a good ear.
          [This is how you see when born not to answer questions
          — Admit what?] He often wept?

       No.

       Go clean yourself up is all she ever said.

OPERA GOD

OPERA GOD

HOLLYWOOD — 1957

No turmoil, no hint of despair spoils the invitation of a fine young face,
or the luxury of a sensuous body that has yet to be worn out from love
being in that bargaining state dreamers use to keep the night alive
when the phone rings, twice . . . then, twice again.

Ah, at last — *the signal* — it's the baritone, the man who uses
the code name Opera God. He has it all arranged.

Sure, she'll make her flight to Copenhagen wearing that powder blue suit,
white gloves, spectator pumps and no jewelry — just pearls
— and she'll ask for zwieback and some ginger ale over the Rockies
until, soon enough, the Pilot used to thinking unnatural things about blondes
will approach her. *It is always a lot smoother up front,* he says.

For him, she will admire the magic of airplanes, muse on the advantages
they have over boats, say how nice it is to know people with pull.

And, as the eel swims for black water,
she, too, will head deeper beneath her future.

COPENHAGEN

The stop-over is brief, the hospital, the room,
                      modern green and meticulous.
It wasn't awful.
It was fresh.

Fresh, the way Opera God would send his plane with the black prancing horse
      emblazoned across its polished chrome tail, his most beautiful
Cavallino Rampante with white suede seats and
on hers, when she enters, she'll see
a red coat box waiting, with its note tucked into a white satin bow
and these words she refuses to read out loud:

> *Ragazza Cara,*
> *I pray you speed me wearing this sable*
> *dreaming in sable of one who loves to give*
> *and receive furry things, too —*
>   *presto, presto, prego!*
>   *OG*

PAVIA

How to explain the way things are for them at the Villa Corso?
They sing, eat giant squid, bathe in Amaretto milk, shaved ice,
hot nights a good applause sends him home to her boiling.
They smoke hashish, drink Moroccan scotch:
    To keep your impressionable soul supple, he says.
    To keep your ah, ah, ah's ignoble, she says.

And, under a ceiling older than Fra Filippo Lippi,
lights from the fountains below breathe up life into cherubim there,
angels akimbo there, doves and glove white lambs there
— The Madonna, that bleeding heart of hers, is up there, too

— center stage — leaking trauma — ubiquitous red tears.

Soon, what is in store feels vast and unknown.
Seems the Cherubim are sniggering.
Seems Madonna's blue bodice oozes trouble. Each morning,
two soggy spots the color of clotted cream start to drip,
never on Opera God, just on her, just before the earth rolls over,
and he prefers to ignore things, or refuses to stop things,
and nobody is stopping at anything anymore.

Seriously — Get it straight. I can't sleep under this
   nightmare the rest of my life, she says.

Nonsense. Every great performance inspires a special birth.
It is age-old. Trust the love, OG says. *Sleep.*

Move the Goddamn bed, she says.

Basta, he says, and puts the ice bucket between their pillows.

What? She says.

To catch the lunacy dripping . . . What's nine months? He says.

[Nine months: Ongoing, onrushing, on fire all the time: Christmas Choruses,
Pietas, Pagliacci, polenta on pounded duck, on paper thin china, post Pope Pius,
post modern hip, the brazen brio, the spinning and swelling

a whole new cosmos — nine months — at the Villa Corso.]

They move into a forward life after Hollywood isn't calling anymore
and what back streets will Opera God roam when she's back home
brooding on the balcony, rubbing her drum-tight stomach with coco
butter, with no clothes on, naked overlooking the Corso's olive groves,
the steeple of the Monarchist's Headquarters in the distance,
its stone public clock rising above the Cypress tops, hands on the damn thing
traipsing after each other for how many hundreds of years
before she decides to read every libretto on earth, falling

       in love with champagne faced coloraturas, licorice haired tenors
(when they are still elevator boys) — Wizardry, that's it, and

       the nonesuch who steer us into our falsehoods
for our art, or, our instant. It was not distasteful —
the taste of certain moments — sunrise,
the villa's gilt double doors opening with the easy fanfare of a brand-new butterfly
— debonair, really, the way a man like Opera God could come back to you,
posh, almost, get on his knees,
offer up the basket of his tanned Promethean hands,

       cradling cannoli swaddled in lemon scented paper;
pouring for you cordials of warm vermouth so sweetly aged
the civilized part of a Sunday might shiver and go writhing.

Straighten up? This is your world. Be here, he'd scold,
throwing open ruby-throated curtains.

     Visualize the cool whoosh of it,

before you a man who knows his legatos, his appoggios,
him softly saying 'yes' to your 'yes'
—Yes, you need more sky? And, here,
Take this sun, this city — feel how they are begging
to be in your blood.

And, whatever temptation shifts a person's fortunes,
 whatever slithering through tatted lace and
 tea-stained linen starched by a Spanish maid confuses the mind,
 it is no wonder really, why an abrupt trip to Italy will shoot down its red
 roots deep, far-reaching as fingerboards to Eden.

SALAMANCA [20 years later]

Nine months, what's nine months so long ago — the musical misfire, her voice
echoing for decades now, siamesed the way two girls were in 1963
dreaming in opposite directions, at war (bound, like that)
when surrender felt so full of everything, and they were feeling so full of
nothing, two girls expecting easy answers, either way,
either on the inside or outside of worlds
— or was it books? And, what was that Spanish maid reading?
How to Marry a Millionaire — *Come Sposare un Millionario.*

The Little Dove, OG called her, carried it in her service cart
in that heap of dirty linen, marinated in tourism and meat sauce
— up and down the rococo halls like cock-a-doodle-do,

up and down the Corso's dumbwaiter — breakfast-lunch-dinner —
taking all the ins and outs any dove would to avert being pecked to death.
Until, before long, is it so mysterious
a maid and her mistress will take steps to abandon Pavia.

Children were involved. *Il Manifesto's* headlines go falling off
   the front pages now. EL ESCANDALO PAVIA CONTINUA.
Big pictures — big type — everything and
   everybody too big to fit inside Opera God's Italy.

And if he hadn't foreseen such trouble, wasn't he amenable
when each had to step from different planes?
Artemis Bligh back in Los Angeles on the arm of her man-on-the-side,
Ferrari, Magdalene Osuna back in Salamanca, alone
reclaimed to the service of her mother, solo in a city not without witchcraft,
a city where a person goes to learn taming and stealing,
and if born to be an artist lives to become an old artist, with fewer appetites,
and she was not unhappy [the Little Dove] when no one gushes
   ooh-lah-lah, and aren't you looking 'sensationale'
   after popping out two baby girls like a little rabbit,

and time is a slow and shamefast animal in Salamanca and
the next twenty years are by no means lackadaisical.

  Look out? [No one could, could they?]

Little Dove would have, and if she could describe it,

she would say the view from her favorite bridge was beautiful *enough* that day,
in the moment an orange sun was coming down tinged toward the violet side,
and on the water below, a square-toed nurse's shoe,
dark glasses, a brown vinyl pocketbook,
pastille foils bobbing like miniature silver buoys,
some Spanish paper money, shells [possibly pistachios] — flotsam
on the ripple deck of a river without much flicker: no gulls,
no truth-tellers, no tender witness for the erstwhile owner it appears,
who was to leave her mess strewn here and
for whom, maybe, right up to the very last breath she is taking,
underestimates her wrath more than her love for the peeled peach light of Pavia,
having lain beneath the moon there, at odds with whether she was dead and
in Heaven, or going the other way for all the right reasons.

A YEAR AFTER THIS...

Near Madrid, a young woman is walking on a bridge,
a masterpiece built by the Moors spanning the Manzanares,
a swift and unusually deep river. Her black, black hair, an amazement of curl
and bravura is what road-weary truckers notice first before they honk.
She is carrying an infant wrapped in a red blanket.
She has not been privy to rumors in Salamanca,
      inside stone houses there,
      inside houses that when you enter, the walls are painted
      retina-searing hues of rosé, peony-pink, medieval shades of umber.

The black haired girl walks here to settle things,

but sees the waves below unfolding as scrolls,

their controversy too easily washing free of them to settle anything.

No matter. She must open a window on the soul.

She expects it not to be so terrible.

Lets her mind slide forward

holding the baby too tightly as it pants, making soft sounds,

tight puffy breaths, but the black haired girl squeezes harder than she should

dreaming of a different way it could have been

had she come to Salamanca as a toddler, in the avocado and pink Pucci romper,

come to be raised here by a mother with one leg shorter than the other,

a mother quite capable of hiking great distances in elevator shoes;

raised by this mother who walked this very bridge,

each day on her way to a factory to paint fake Goyas,

a factory belonging to the family of a lover she had once,

a widower derided for his lisp that evaded the *th*-sound

   of the Castilian terminal *z* : Awkward man, awkward

thoughts at precisely the moment a couple approaches from behind,

their emaciated Mastiff on a ratty blue nylon rope smells vaguely of skunk.

The two are disheveled, gesticulating, the woman smoking her cigarette,

   points at the bridge turrets, then to the river below,

   her arm like a scarf caught in the door of a speeding car,

the stench from that cigarette making the black-haired girl feel superior,

and she'll stop, pull the baby's cap over its face, until the couple can walk

ahead.

Except, they don't get far. They don't get thirty feet before stopping

— they just stop, heave the dog over the side, turning back, not caring

to see where it hits, walking back to wherever they are from,
like this act was about going nowhere to do nothing,
and the young woman's veins fill with sugar.

No. She has not come here to let them be her business
          and focuses on the baby now. Unable to face the river anymore
she squats, leans against the filigreed grillwork, iron rosettes pushing icy
imprints into the flesh of her slender back
          nothing changing the confusion or the orderliness,
the traffic is still the blood on its journey back to some heart
where drivers do not notice when a girl puts a baby wrapped in a red fleece bunting
     down on the dirty cement of a bridge,
or if a girl loses more of her thinking under a cloudless cerulean sky,
this blue, the same blue as the eyes threading three generations of women,
one to another, until, in this place, right here,
     is it possible motorists think of creatures by the wayside
they've ignored before, the ones that skitter out of some impracticality,
caught so far outside the firmament of their own purpose
[like larvae feeding on plant lice] fret over fresh pastries
and cut off hours at the bank, more than babies cast to the ground
. . . and when that couple passes by the girl and the child again,
the man is asking the woman if she thinks the dog will sink,
get caught in debris at the bottom.

"No, no," she answers, waving that wild cigarette hand of hers,
nasty currents.

ABOUT THE AUTHOR

JOAN STEPP SMITH is a native San Franciscan. She divides her time between California and Montana where she works with horses in the Bitterroot Valley.